100 THINGS TO DO IN MEMPHIS BEFORE YOU DIE

4th Edition

Memphis from the water
Photo courtesy of Antony-22,
Wikimedia Commons

100 THINGS TO DO IN MEMPHIS BEFORE YOU DIE

4th Edition

HOLLY R. WHITFIELD

REEDY PRESS

Reedy Press
PO Box 5131
St. Louis, MO 63139, USA
www.reedypress.com

Library of Congress Control Number: 2022936990

ISBN: 9781681063881

Design by Jill Halpin

Unless otherwise indicated, all photos are in the public domain.

Printed in the United States of America
24 25 26 27 28 5 4 3 2 1

DEDICATION

For my family and friends.

And for the people who still read books.

Beale Street
Photo courtesy of Unsplash

CONTENTS

Music and Entertainment

Sports and Recreation

Culture and History

Mud Island Park
Photo courtesy of AlexisRosendahl,
Wikimedia Commons

ACKNOWLEDGMENTS

To Memphis for being unapologetically what you are, and Memphians for always sharing stories.

To my colleagues past and present.

To Reedy Press for offering the privilege to write about Memphis.

To Samantha Crespo, not only for creating the first three editions of this book but for giving me the blessing to carry on the project and for encouragement, in general.

To all my friends, family, loved ones, and the readers.

I Am a Man mural
Photo courtesy of Unsplash

PREFACE

Welcome to the fourth edition of *100 Things to Do in Memphis Before You Die*, a decade after author and my fellow Memphis lover Samantha Crespo penned the first edition.

Much has changed in Memphis—and the world—since then. Places that were merely plans and dreams back then have been built and become established firmly in the city's landscape as must-dos and must-sees. Neighborhoods have grown, new venues have popped up, beloved restaurants have closed, and exciting, new favorites have opened their doors. Most of what's included in the following pages is different from past editions, and all of it has been revisited, rewritten, and re-researched.

This edition reflects, as best as I can, today's Memphis and what I think visitors, newcomers and longtime residents should make sure they experience, whether they have a few hours or 100 years in the Bluff City.

Some of the items are obvious; some are a little more obscure. This book is meant as an introduction to Memphis, but it has some deeper cuts that I hope will serve those who already know and love the city. Know that Memphis is an endless well of culture, art, and experiences that could never be contained in any number of volumes.

Changes to locations and events were happening in real time as I was writing this book, but the information is as up-to-date as it could be at the time of publication. Be sure to call ahead and do some research before you strike out to check out these activities in person. You can also visit secretmemphis.com and @secretmemphis on social media for updates.

I hope you *do* decide to venture out in “real life” to experience whatever strikes your fancy or arouses your curiosity. In a world where it’s easy to scroll and experience life virtually, committing to in-person experiences can be surprisingly fun, refreshing, and valuable. Tell ’em I sent you!

—Holly R. Whitfield

Elvis Presley's pink Cadillac
Photo courtesy of Unsplash

Central BBQ
Photo courtesy of Flickr Commons

FOOD AND DRINK

1

BEGIN YOUR DAY
THE MEMPHIS WAY

Brother Juniper's is a Memphis classic in the University of Memphis area that hits all the breakfast benchmarks. Families pack it out on weekends to enjoy the cozy, casual atmosphere and friendly service. The café is known for their San Diegan open-faced omelet, stuffed with sautéed mushrooms, tomatoes, bacon, and feta, and served with home fries. Brother Juniper's famous cinnamon roll pancakes are another mouthwatering way to start the day. If neither of those options floats your boat, try one of the egg scrambles or breakfast burritos, and wash it down with a mug of fresh coffee.

You might also want to try The Liquor Store's brunchy all-day breakfast menu of diner-inspired dishes with a Latin flair. Another delicious breakfast option is Sunrise restaurant, which serves Bloody Marys, breakfast bowls, and the popular "Rooster" fried chicken thigh biscuit.

Brother Juniper's
3519 Walker Ave.
901-324-0144
brotherjunipers.com

The Liquor Store
2655 Broad Ave.
669 S Mendenhall Rd.
901-405-5477
thebroadliquorstore.com

Sunrise
670 Jefferson Ave.
901-552-3168
5469 Poplar Ave.
901-844-6117
sunrise901.com

TIP

There can be a wait on the weekend, so plan to go early or have Brother Juniper's breakfast on a weekday morning to avoid a line.

2

FUEL UP WITH COFFEE
AT VICE & VIRTUE

In the lobby of the ARRIVE hotel on South Main you'll find local micro-batch coffee roaster Vice & Virtue serving up specialty coffees and espresso. Try the bourbon-barrel-aged espresso in their signature bourbon mocha drink, or grab a matcha latte to enjoy while you work at a community table or settle into a cozy chair. The hotel's in-house bakery Hustle & Dough serves pastries and fresh-baked bread for avocado toast or by the loaf.

Need a java jolt before your trip to Graceland? Muggin Coffeehouse in Uptown has plenty of Memphis personality with drinks like the white-mocha-inspired Zippin Pippin on the menu, named after Elvis' favorite Memphis roller coaster.

Downtowners seeking caffeine and a place to hang find both at Comeback Coffee near the Pyramid, with coffee, specialty espresso-based drinks, and their signature coffee sodas.

Vice & Virtue / Hustle & Dough
477 S Main St.
901-701-7577
vicevirtuecoffee.com

Muggin Coffeehouse
606 N Main St.
901-529-7759
muggincoffeehouse.com

Comeback Coffee
358 N Main St.
901-860-4215
comebackcoffeeus.com

3

CUE IT UP:
MEMPHIS BARBECUE PICKS

Someone once said, "Everyone in Memphis has a different favorite BBQ joint, and they're all correct." Try them all, and decide for yourself. Start out at Payne's, which for 50 years has served some of the best Memphis barbecue in town. Don't let the unassuming concrete building and hole-in-the-wall vibes fool you; Payne's Bar-B-Q has lots of local cred. Order the pulled pork sandwich topped with their tangy mustard slaw or a rack of ribs to start, with a smoked sausage if you're still hungry.

Next, head Downtown to Cozy Corner for delectable ribs and BBQ Cornish hens. The restaurant is owned by Desiree Robinson, the first Black woman pitmaster to be inducted into the American Royal's Barbecue Hall of Fame. Then follow the smoke and aromas down the Downtown alley to the best-known barbecue joint in town, the Rendezvous, where you can feast on charbroiled pork ribs coated in a Greek spice dry rub.

Payne's Bar-B-Q
1762 Lamar Ave.
901-272-1523
facebook.com/paynesbbqmemphis

Cozy Corner
735 N Pkwy.
901-527-9158
cozycornerbbq.com

Rendezvous
52 S 2nd St.
901-523-2746
hogsfly.com

TIP

If you go to the World Championship Barbecue Cooking Contest held each May, be sure you purchase a ticket to Kingsford Tour of Champions or BBQ Alley. Otherwise (unless you know someone on a competition team) you won't be able to sample the barbecue.

REMIX A CLASSIC:
UNIQUE MEMPHIS BARBECUE

Continue your tour of Memphis barbecue favorites, but with a twist. It makes you wonder, what wouldn't Memphians put barbecue on? At Central BBQ, they put their slow-smoked pulled pork on barbecue nachos, which the locals order with house-made potato chips or even fries. Central began as a Memphis in May competition team, but now they've expanded across the southeast.

Another beloved local spot for barbecue in all its forms, the Bar-B-Q Shop claims to have invented Bar-B-Q spaghetti—pork shoulder and a secret recipe of barbecue tomato sauce over pasta. Order it as a side to your ribs or sandwich (served on Texas Toast). Horest Coletta introduced Memphis to the barbecue pizza in the 1950s, when it was popular with sailors from the nearby naval base, Elvis Presley himself, and eventually, everybody. You can sit in the Elvis room at the Coletta's South Parkway location and try some for yourself.

Central BBQ
Multiple locations
eatcbq.com

The Bar-B-Q Shop
1782 Madison Ave.
901-272-1277
thebar-b-qshop.com

Coletta's Italian Restaurant
1063 S Pkwy. E
901-948-7652
colettas.net

TIP

If you're looking for Memphis's favorite hot wings (see #6), Central BBQ's smoked chicken wings are at the top of many locals' lists.

NOURISH YOUR SPIRIT
WITH THESE SOUL FOOD SIGNATURES

You can taste the love at Memphis's favorite soul food restaurants, where macaroni and cheese is considered a vegetable and the tea is sweet enough you won't need dessert (but you'll want it!).

The Four Way

The historic Four Way restaurant has anchored the Soulsville neighborhood for decades and has served dignitaries from Martin Luther King Jr. to Elvis Presley to President Barack Obama. But what keeps the locals coming back is the incredible food and amazing hospitality. A few of your options: chicken, catfish, salmon croquettes, turkey and dressing, plus a slew of tasty Southern sides.

998 Mississippi Blvd.
901-507-1519
fourway901.com

Alcenia's

Owner B.J. Chester-Tamayo will greet you (or send you off) with a big hug, so bring an open heart to Alcenia's along with a big appetite and a little extra time. Every plate piled high with classics like fried chicken or meatloaf is made fresh to order in the small kitchen. Alcenia's had a full renovation in 2022 in the original building near the Bass Pro Pyramid.

317 N Main St.
901-523-0200
alcenias.com

6

PUT A WING ON IT
WITH MEMPHIS HOT WINGS

What's the best-known food in Memphis? It's a trick question, because while the slow-smoked pork of Memphis barbecue is world famous, our hot wings are legendary. There are more chicken wing joints than you can shake a leg at, but two places to get you started are the Wing Guru and New Wing Order.

Started by former Memphis Tigers basketball player Billy Richmond Jr., local chain the Wing Guru prides itself on perfectly cooked wings with plenty of sauce options, including Guru Gold, their take on the sweet-but-tangy Memphis honey gold sauce. Pick your heat level on any flavor from mild to "insane."

After a few wins at the World Championship Hot Wing Contest, New Wing Order owners opened their own food truck (and later, added a restaurant on Beale Street) specializing in award-winning flavors like Memphis Buffalo, Mud Island Jerk, and the super spicy Ring of Fire.

The Wing Guru
Multiple locations
thewingguru.com

New Wing Order
341 Beale St.
901-747-8893
newwingorder.com

7

TASTE THE SWEET AND SPICY LOVE
AT UNCLE LOU'S FRIED CHICKEN

This Memphis chicken spot might be in a no-frills strip mall in Whitehaven, but the food is anything but ordinary. Most people associate Memphis fried chicken with Gus's, which is well-deserved and worth visiting for sure. But once you've had Gus's (they have locations all over the country) it's time to try a little of Lou's sweet 'n' spicy love. Prepare before you go, so you know what to order when you make it to the counter; sometimes there's a line, but the food comes out fast and piping hot. Decide how many pieces, white or dark meat, and which level of spice you desire. But whatever you do, don't expect Nashville Hot Chicken doused in oil here. At Uncle Lou's, the flavor is marinated in—from the juicy, tender meat through the crispy, seasoned skin for each addicting, satisfying bite. Don't forget the honey butter biscuits.

3633 Millbranch Rd.
901-332-2367
unclelousfriedchicken.com

MUNCH ON BURGERS AND FRITTERS
AT SHELBY FOREST GENERAL STORE

The decor is down-home Southern cabin themed, with taxidermy, antlers, and memorabilia on the walls, and the menu is simple: cheeseburgers, corn fritters. But there's nothing better than a stop at the Shelby Forest General Store after a day at Meeman-Shelby Forest State Park working up an appetite. If you need provisions for your outdoor adventure, they're stocked with all the necessities like snacks, beer, ice, fried pies, live bait, firewood, and even discs for the nearby disc golf course. The owners, Doug and Kristin Ammons, will treat you like family at this Millington institution. Sit outside and enjoy your meal fresh from the griddle. The General Store is open Monday through Thursday, 11 a.m. to 2 p.m., and on Fridays, Saturdays, and Sundays 6 a.m. to 4 p.m. Just be sure you get there on time; the grill shuts down 30 minutes before closing time.

7729 Benjestown Rd., Millington
901-876-5770
shelbyforestgeneralstore.com

9

FIND YOUR INNER FOODIE
AT ACRE

If you're not looking for ACRE restaurant in East Memphis, you might easily pass by the quaint, cozy, surprisingly quiet spot off South Perkins Street near the botanic garden. The sophisticated decor sets the backdrop for a dining experience that feels at once elevated and welcoming. There's also a courtyard charming enough to host weddings and special events.

Mississippi native and longtime Memphis chef Wally Joe's dedication to fresh, seasonal ingredients and rich, varied flavors carries through the menu—which is set up for traditional appetizer and entrée meals or a small-plates-sharing experience. Signature dishes include the red snapper served whole and lightly battered, with a mouthwatering ponzu sauce, and roasted baby carrots with thick labneh, walnuts, and spices.

690 S Perkins Rd.
901-818-2273
acrememphis.com

10

DINE AROUND THE WORLD
AT GLOBAL CAFÉ

Global Café in the Crosstown Concourse (see #78) offers traditional food prepared by refugees from different countries, and frequently changes the menu so there's always something new to try. There are at least three food stands to choose from—past countries represented include Syria, Argentina, Korea, Nepal, Jamaica, and more.

Go for a spicy Sudanese African peanut soup or Somali spaghetti (made with a mix of peppers, onions, tomato sauce, noodles, and fried plantains), or an order of Mexican carnitas street tacos. Best of all, you don't have to choose just one style of cuisine to sample. If you have the appetite, order a Venezuelan arepa with a side of falafel and hummus, or the Sudanese sambusa (pastry filled with beef or vegetables) and albondigas (Venezuelan meatballs).

The casual spot has a full bar with regular margarita specials, including the mango-rita, a mango flavored margarita topped with a full mango carved into a rose.

1350 Concourse Ave., Ste. 157
901-512-6890
globalcafememphis.com

11

ENJOY
PLANT-BASED DISHES

If you enjoy a plant-based diet or just want to go meat free for a meal, Memphis actually does have some options for vegetarians and vegans. City Silo Table + Pantry offers a menu that accommodates vegan, vegetarian, or omnivore palates with customizable sandwiches, bowls, and salads. Try the Buffalo tempeh and sesame cauliflower bowl with cashew ranch for a flavorful, protein-packed lunch. Round out your meal with a smoothie or fresh-pressed juice.

For vegan comfort food at its finest, go to Plant Based Heat near the University of Memphis for cauliflower "wings," seasoned Beyond Meat burgers, or crispy oyster mushroom sandwiches. Imagine Vegan Cafe in Cooper Young serves up vegan versions of Southern eats, including Memphis-style "BBQ."

TIP

Follow the Vegan Crunk blog at vegancrunk.blogspot.com, where *Cookin' Crunk: Eatin' Vegan in the Dirty South* author Bianca Phillips shares vegan dining experiences in Memphis.

City Silo Table + Pantry
5101 Sanderlin Ave., Ste. 104
901-729-7687

7605 W Farmington Blvd., Ste. 2, Germantown
901-236-7223
thecitysilo.com

Plant Based Heat
669 S Highland St.
plantbasedheat.com

Imagine Vegan Cafe
2158 Young Ave.
901-654-3455

12

TAKE
A SUMMER AVENUE TOUR

Summer Avenue is home to a plethora of Memphis restaurant stalwarts, from breakfast to barbecue to tacos to dim sum. At Elwood's Shack, popular dishes include barbecue, fish tacos, pimento cheese biscuits, a delicious roast beef "debris" po-boy, and smoked hot dogs. The Shack Attack platter lets you sample ribs, pulled pork, brisket, smoked sausage, and smoked chicken legs, served with sides. The small restaurant's original location is in an actual shack in the Lowe's parking lot.

Also on Summer Avenue, Bryant's Breakfast offers perfect Southern biscuits (with gravy, or sausage, or sausage gravy) or a hearty breakfast platter. Taqueria La Guadalupana serves traditional Mexican dishes, tortas, and street tacos (filling options include beef, pork, goat, tongue, and more). At Dim Sum King, eat authentic Chinese dishes including all the dumplings, noodles, and snacks you can sample from the dim sum cart daily.

Elwood's Shack
4523 Summer Ave.

4040 Park Ave.
901-761-9898
elwoodsshack.com

Bryant's Breakfast
3965 Summer Ave.
901-324-7494
bryantsbreakfast.com

Taqueria La Guadalupana
4818 Summer Ave.
901-685-6857
guadalupanamemphis.com

Dim Sum King
5266 Summer Ave.
901-766-0831
dimsumkingmemphis.com

CONSTRUCT THE ANTIPASTI COURSE OF YOUR DREAMS

AT BARI

Offering fresh, seasonal Southeastern Italian cuisine, Bari Ristorante e Enoteca has been a Memphis favorite since 2002. Owned by husband-and-wife team Jason and Rebecca Severs, Bari offers fresh seafood, imported cheeses, house-made pastas, fine wines, and some of the best cocktails in town.

You can start with a series of small plates for the perfect antipasti course, choosing from a selection of more than 50 cheeses, gourmet salami and prosciutto, marinated and grilled vegetables, and oysters, calamari, or anchovies.

Venture into the pasta section next for Bari's signature carbonara or the orzo con pomodoro e granchio—tender orzo in a tomato sauce with lump crab—before continuing on to more fish and meat dishes. Finish off with sweet desserts or have another cheese course with your after-dinner drinks.

524 S Cooper St.
901-722-2244
barimemphis.com

TIP

Make reservations in advance for the dining room or patio, or arrive early for a seat at the bar.

14

SIP PILSNERS, STOUTS, AND MORE
AT WISEACRE BREWING

Memphis water is famously considered some of the best tasting in the world. Its pure, neutral, ever-so-slightly sweet taste comes from filtration through layers of our 40-million-year-old underground sands aquifer. This tasty water is what Memphis's many local breweries use for their award-winning craft beers. Sample them at pubs in town, or visit a taproom—most offer indoor and outdoor seating, specialty brews, and fun activities in a dog- and kid-friendly environment.

Founded by brothers Davin and Kellan Bartosch in 2013, Wiseacre Brewing opened a taproom on Broad Avenue that same year. After several years of winning beer competitions and winning over crowds of thirsty beer lovers at that location, Wiseacre debuted their new headquarters Downtown in 2020. Both taprooms have sprawling patios and a range of tasty brews, from the classic Tiny Bomb American pilsner to the Memphis Sands lager (named for the water source, of course) to the popular Gotta Get Up to Get Down coffee stout.

Wiseacre Broad
2783 Broad Ave.

Wiseacre HQ
398 S B.B. King Blvd.

wiseacrebrew.com

TIP

Wiseacre's Broad Avenue location hosts different food trucks, and their Downtown spot is home to Little Bettie pizza joint. The pups have to stay outside at the Downtown location.

15

TASTE MEMPHIS HISTORY
AT OLD DOMINICK DISTILLERY

Crafted directly from the recipe of first-generation Italian immigrant Domenico Canale, the new Old Dominick Hot Toddy whiskey is a taste of Memphis history. In 2013, Domenico's descendants Chris and Alex Canale discovered an unopened bottle of Toddy from the late 1800s and were inspired to reinstate the brand and build the city's first modern-day distillery in the heart of Downtown Memphis.

In 2017 they hired Alex Castle, the first woman master distiller in the state of Tennessee, to helm the spirit-making process starting with vodkas and gins, including the tangerine-and-grapefruit-infused Honeybell Citrus vodka. Today you can visit the distillery for a behind-the-scenes look at the distilling process, sample spirits in the tasting room, and even enjoy the sunset on the rooftop. In 2022, Old Dominick released the first official five-year-aged Tennessee whiskey made in the city of Memphis since Prohibition.

305 S Front St.
901-260-1250
olddominick.com

16

INDULGE YOUR TASTE BUDS

AT MUDDY'S BAKE SHOP

From their adorable bakery on Broad Avenue, Muddy's Bake Shop founder Kat Gordon and the "gnomies" (bakers) spread love and delicious fresh-baked treats across the Memphis area. Locals have lined up for Muddy's treats, including the "Prozac" cupcake (that's a devil's food chocolate cake with chocolate buttercream icing) and the classic Plain Jane (gourmet vanilla cake and vanilla frosting) since the doors opened on Leap Day in 2008.

If pies are more your thing, the chocolate chess Cocoa Crackle pie has a fudgy filling and a thin "crust" on top, all in a buttery, flaky pie crust; there are also plenty of cookies, bars, and oatmeal cream pies to fulfill every flavor of indulgence. You can order your treats ahead of time, or visit the lovely neighborhood bakery to shop the shelves.

2497 Broad Ave.
901-683-8844
muddysbakeshop.com

17

CHOOSE A CLASSIC OR A SUPREME

AT JERRY'S

Any day of the year, you'll find people lined up outside a small building in Memphis's Berclair neighborhood as they've been doing since the 1960s. The stand is painted bubblegum pink with green and yellow trim; a polka-dotted polar bear statue and a giant ice cream cone sculpture sit on the roof—you can't miss Jerry's Sno Cones. There are tons of flavors to choose from. You can go with a classic Tiger's Blood, Wedding Cake, or watermelon, or venture out with a bright green Ninja Turtle, Mango Tango, or a fruity Hurricane Elvis.

And at Jerry's, you can make it "a supreme"! This means they'll layer soft serve vanilla between delectable scoops of flavored shaved ice. The newer location in Cordova also boasts the signature pink exterior, and has indoor and outdoor seating.

1657 Wells Station Rd.
901-767-2659

1601 Bonnie Ln., Cordova
901-249-8718
jerryssnowcones.com

TIP

Don't underestimate the burgers, corn nuggets, and funnel cakes from the hot foods menu.

18

GET A TASTE OF NEW ORLEANS
AT RESTAURANT IRIS

Memphis entered a new culinary era in 2008 when Chef Kelly English opened Restaurant Iris in a cozy, upscale little spot in Midtown. A Louisiana native trained in New Orleans, English and his team offer a menu influenced by Southern, Creole, and French cuisines. Dishes like the lobster knuckle sandwich and the steak stuffed with fried oysters earned Iris a spot in Memphians' hearts. In 2009, English was named *Food & Wine* magazine's "Best New Chef" and a few years later, he opened the Second Line next door, a casual bar known for po' boys, BBQ shrimp, and an excellent patio.

Today, Restaurant Iris operates out of a larger spot in East Memphis with a booth-filled dining room and a well-appointed bar—where you can still get that lobster knuckle sandwich. Go there for lunch, dinner, or brunch for delicious dishes like smoked duck gumbo, lobster crepes, boudin-stuffed quail, crawfish étouffée, and fried green tomatoes.

TIP

The Second Line is still open in its original location and another Kelly English team concept, Swamp Bar, offers global creole fusion cuisine and cocktails in the former Iris space.

Restaurant Iris
4550 Poplar Ave.
901-590-2828
restaurantiris.com

The Second Line
2144 Monroe Ave.
901-590-2829
secondlinememphis.com

Swamp Bar
2146 Monroe Ave.
901-417-7491

SIP SOMETHING SPECIAL
AT CAMEO

In 2022, some longtime Memphis bartenders combined their passion for inventive cocktails and great vibes to open Cameo bar in Midtown. Vintage-style portraits and mounted taxidermy adorn the hunter-green walls, and a delicate arrangement of sculpted light bulbs hang above the long bar, creating an eccentric but cozy atmosphere.

Guests order from a leather-bound booklet full of classic cocktails like gin fizzes, sours, martinis, and mocktails. The must-drink experience comes from the seasonal house cocktail menu, though, where you'll find something for every taste: herbal, aromatic, fruity, sweet, refreshing, or tart. Owners Mary Oglesby and Paul Gilliam plan a variety of dinners, drag shows, movie nights, and Packers watch parties to keep things lively. That, plus tongue-in-cheek drink names like "Season Tickets to Dollywood" and "Cinematic Vampire Violence," means Cameo's slogan "Fancy Drinks, Party Time" makes a lot of sense.

1835 Union Ave., Ste. 103
901-305-6911
cameomemphis.com

TIP

Visit on a Tuesday, when Cameo's team brings out the Mardi Gras beads and turns on the New Orleans tunes for weekly Fat Tuesday specials like hurricanes, sazeracs, po'boys and gumbo.

20

SPEND A FRUITFUL DAY
AT JONES ORCHARD

Head out to the orchard to pick your own fruit at Jones Orchard, about 10 miles north of Memphis. While you can certainly find locally grown produce, including Jones Orchard's, at area farmers markets, there's something special about spending a spring day gathering strawberries or grabbing your own juicy peaches straight from the tree. In the fall, Jones Orchard has a bountiful pumpkin patch, plenty of fall vegetables and a haunted corn maze for Halloween.

They offer two pick-your-own locations and a crop calendar on their website so you can look forward to strawberries, blackberries, peaches, plums, nectarines, pears, and pumpkin season throughout the year. The adjacent farm stands offer plenty of prepicked fruits and vegetables, plus jams, jellies, and relishes straight from the farm.

Jones Farm Market
7170 Hwy. 51 N, Millington
901-873-3150

Big Creek Pick-Your-Own
6824 Big Creek Church Rd., Millington

jonesorchard.com

SEE MEMPHIS
WITH A VIEW FROM THE TOP

In Memphis, you can party on the top floor of the city's most iconic buildings. The most famous rooftop is that of the Peabody Memphis hotel, where the annual summer party series has been going strong since 1939. Every Thursday from April through August, partygoers pack the rooftop of the luxury hotel for live music or DJs, food, and free-flowing drinks as the sun sets over Downtown's skyline.

Downtown, there's also the Beck & Call lounge on top of the Hyatt Centric, with an incredible view of the iconic Hernando de Soto Bridge and craft cocktails; the Mississippi Terrace at the Pyramid hosts monthly parties at the riverside landmark. In Midtown, the Memphian hotel's Tiger and Peacock overlooks Overton Square and has a snazzy lounge, a private champagne room, and a rooftop patio.

The Peabody Memphis
149 Union Ave.
901-529-4000
peabodymemphis.com

Beck & Call at Hyatt Centric
33 Beale St.
901-403-5320
beckandcallmemphis.com

Mississippi Terrace
at Big Cypress Lodge (Pyramid)
1 Bass Pro Dr.
800-223-3333
big-cypress.com

Tiger and Peacock
at the Memphian
21 S Cooper St.
901-538-7313
tigerandpeacockmemphis.com

TIP

Rooftop hours may vary, and some have a dress code. Call ahead for information.

22

FEAST
AT THESE FINE DINING FAVORITES

From French cuisine and handmade pastas to wood-fired pizzas and standout cocktails and wines, Memphis chefs Andrew Ticer and Michael Hudman's restaurant group has something for everyone.

One of their restaurants, Catherine & Mary's, is located in the historic Chisca on Main building Downtown. The modern atmosphere with a long bar and table seating make the restaurant perfect for after-work drinks, date nights, or celebratory dinners. The rustic but refined Italian menu offers handmade pastas, like the rigatoni with "Maw Maw's" gravy or radiatore cacio e pepe, and hearty pork and steak entrées.

Their first restaurant, the cozy Andrew Michael Italian Kitchen, is in East Memphis across the street from the casual (but still upscale) Hog & Hominy, a drinks and wood-fired pizza hot spot. In the Central Station hotel Downtown, try classic French dishes at Ticer and Hudman's Bishop restaurant; grab a drink from Eight & Sand stand in the lobby.

Catherine & Mary's
272 S Main St., Ste. 105-A
901-254-8600
catherineandmarys.com

Andrew Michael Italian Kitchen
712 W Brookhaven Cir.
901-347-3569
andrewmichaelitaliankitchen.com

Hog & Hominy
707 W Brookhaven Cir.
901-779-6096
hogandhominy.com

Bishop
545 S Main St., Ste. 111
901-896-0228
bishopmemphis.com

Eight & Sand
545 S Main St.
901-524-5247
centralstationmemphis.com/food-drink

For more information on the restaurant group, visit enjoyam.com

B.B. King's Blues Club
Courtesy of Unsplash

MUSIC AND ENTERTAINMENT

23

HEAR RARE SONGS
AT THE BLUES HALL OF FAME

Since 1980, the Memphis-based Blues Foundation has maintained a rich catalog of sound recordings, writings, photographs, and artifacts chronicling the blues as an international music phenomenon.

The foundation also inducts musicians and other professionals into the Blues Hall of Fame, honoring more than 400 individuals since it began.

In 2015 the foundation opened a physical location for the Blues Hall of Fame, an interactive museum and gallery in Downtown Memphis dedicated to showcase the stories of blues musicians, their lives, and work.

Each section has a large touchscreen for visitors to dig deeper on their pilgrimages. It's a chance to listen to songs that can't be heard anywhere else.

421 S Main St.
901-527-2583
blues.org

TIP

Across the street from the National Civil Rights Museum, an hour-long visit to the Blues Hall of Fame is part of a day exploring the South Main District.

HONOR A SUPERSTAR
AT GRACELAND

It's the second-most-visited home in the United States, and Memphis's most famous landmark: Graceland. As the family home of worldwide superstar Elvis Presley, the house—officially called "The Mansion"—is now the centerpiece of a collection of attractions that bring thousands of Elvis fans and music lovers to Memphis from across the globe.

The Meditation Garden adjacent to the Mansion is also the final resting place for several members of the Presley family, including Elvis, his parents, and his daughter, Lisa Marie Presley. The gates of Graceland are open at no charge each morning from 7:30 to 8:30 a.m. so that visitors may pay their respects.

In addition to the house, guests can visit the car museum, exhibition spaces, restaurants, and even tour Elvis's private jets. The Guest House at Graceland hotel nearby hosts events throughout the year, including Elvis Tribute Artist competitions. The Soundstage at Graceland is a venue on-site that hosts nationally touring bands and big-name comedians.

3717 Elvis Presley Blvd.
901-332-3322
graceland.com

FEEL THE MOJO
AT THE MEMPHIS MUSIC HALL OF FAME AND THE ROCK 'N' SOUL MUSEUM

There's much more to Memphis music than Elvis, and you can experience the full picture of the city's musical heritage and current artists at a pair of museums just off of Beale Street in Downtown Memphis. An affiliate of the Smithsonian, the Memphis Rock 'n' Soul Museum highlights the origins of rock and blues through recorded oral histories, songs, photos, and artifacts. See the original lyric sheet for "Heartbreak Hotel" and Ike Turner's first piano, and hear music from undersung heroes like Sister Rosetta Tharpe and Robert Johnson.

Around the corner at the Memphis Music Hall of Fame, check out a small but impactful collection of items representing the hundreds of artists that the Hall of Fame has honored since its inception in 2012. On display you'll find Three 6 Mafia's Best Original Song Oscar award, part of Jerry Lee Lewis's custom Cadillac, and numerous costumes worn by Memphis music dignitaries.

Memphis Rock 'n' Soul Museum
191 Beale St.
901-205-2533
memphisrocknsoul.org

Memphis Music Hall of Fame
126 Beale St.
901-205-2532
memphismusichalloffame.com

TIP

Get a combination ticket to both museums for a discounted rate.

EXPLORE GOSPEL ROOTS
AT THE STAX MUSEUM

If you don't know the Stax name, you certainly know the Stax sound. Otis Redding's "(Sittin' On) The Dock of the Bay," Sam & Dave's "Hold On! I'm Comin'," and Isaac Hayes's *Hot Buttered Soul* album were all recorded and released on the Stax record label in the '60s and '70s in a south Memphis neighborhood now dubbed "Soulsville USA."

Visit the Stax Museum of American Soul Music, rebuilt from the rubble of the razed original building that housed the studio and record shop. Start with a film that shares the tumultuous history of the label, then walk through a series of exhibits that explore soul music's gospel roots and the heyday of Stax's hit songs.

Despite the ups and downs of the label's history, Stax's fun vibe comes through in the museum's Soul Train dance floor, and Isaac Hayes's spinning gold-plated, fur-lined Cadillac.

926 E McLemore Ave.
901-261-6338
staxmuseum.com

TIP

Spend time at Stax's Satellite Record and Gift Shop after your tour.

27

VISIT THE BIRTHPLACE OF ROCK AND ROLL AT SUN STUDIO

The funky triangular building at the corner of Union Avenue and Marshall Avenue in Downtown Memphis is eye-catching now but must have been unassuming in the 1950s when a young Elvis Presley first approached the Memphis Recording Studio to lay down vocals as a birthday present for his mother.

Better known as Sun Studio, the site is where four music legends convened on a fateful day in 1956 for the infamous "Million Dollar Quartet" photo. Elvis Presley, Johnny Cash, Carl Perkins, and Jerry Lee Lewis all recorded tracks at the studio early in their careers.

Sam Phillips founded the studio in 1952 and today, guests can take a lively tour led by local Memphis musicians who are passionate about Sun's storied history.

706 Union Ave.
901-521-0664
sunstudio.com

TIP

Tickets must be purchased in person on the day of the tour, so stop by Sun Studio when they open to reserve your time, and plan to return later in the day.

MINGLE THE NIGHT AWAY
ON BEALE STREET

The historic "Home of the Blues," this neon-lit boulevard in Downtown Memphis is lined with clubs, venues, and shops for a full night of music, drinks, and merriment.

The best way to "do" Beale Street is to let the music guide you. You might catch a blues act at B.B. King's Blues Club, a soul cover band at Rum Boogie Cafe, or a free outdoor concert in Handy Park. Silky O'Sullivan's pub boasts a spacious patio with live music, and Ghost River Brewing Co.'s taproom offers local beer and irresistible Memphis hot wings from the award-winning New Wing Order restaurant.

Rum Boogie Cafe
182 Beale St.
901-528-0150
rumboogie.com

B.B. King's Blues Club
143 Beale St.
901-524-5464
bbkings.com/memphis

FUN FACT

Beale Street is the only location in the state of Tennessee where it's legal to carry an open alcoholic beverage. Grab yourself a to-go drink and stroll down the street, which is perfect for people-watching and mingling, especially before a Memphis Grizzlies game.

PACK IN FOR A SHOW
AT BAR DKDC

For local flavor in the form of eclectic music and cold drinks, sidle up at Bar DKDC in the Cooper-Young neighborhood. Colorful folk art adorns the walls in contrast with metallic modern fixtures and mood lighting. There's a vintage photo booth for group pictures and cozy, curtained nooks for sharing plates of international street food and cocktails served in mason jars.

A couple nights a week around 8 or 9 p.m., local bands set up in the dining room and turn up the tunes until late in the evening. You might catch soul-infused rock group The Sheiks, zydeco songstress Marcella Simien, or the Lucky 7 Brass Band, to name a few.

Bar DKDC, which reportedly stands for "don't know, don't care," is owned by Memphis restaurateur and chef Karen Carrier, who also owns The Beauty Shop restaurant next door.

964 S Cooper St.
901-272-0830
bardkdc.com

30

DINE AND DANCE
AT LAFAYETTE'S MUSIC ROOM

The original Lafayette's Music Room was a staple of the Square in the 1970s, when the district was the hottest party spot in the city. Memphians of a certain age will tell you about seeing Billy Joel and other big names on stage at Lafayette's when they were relatively unknown. By the mid-'80s the area went dark as businesses closed and times changed. In 2012 Overton Square was revitalized, including this music spot.

These days, the double-decker venue hosts live bands every night, and twice on Sundays. Catch local groups and national touring acts, including bluegrass music for weekend brunch. There's a Southern Creole menu, good drinks, and warm breezes on the second-story patio.

2119 Madison Ave.
901-207-5097
lafayettes.com

LISTEN TO FREE-FLOWING MUSIC
AT THE OVERTON PARK SHELL

Memphis evenings in summer and fall mean free live music at the Overton Park Shell outdoor amphitheater. Save a bundle on concert tickets and concessions by attending one of the music venue's dozens of free events every year and packing a picnic or cooler. Locals gather by the hundreds to enjoy a variety of music genres including jazz, soul, fusion, and funk while they lounge on blankets or sit in chairs on the lawn. There are food trucks and a cash bar on-site, too. The Overton Park Shell is one of 27 shell-shaped stages built with WPA assistance in 1936, one of the last in the country still standing. Everyone from Elvis Presley (who played his first-ever public show at the Shell) to the Grateful Dead to Mavis Staples have performed, so you'll be getting a piece of history along with your evening of free live music.

1928 Poplar Ave.
901-300-3011
overtonparkshell.org

TIP

Go online to book the Backstage Experience Tour at the Shell, a museum behind the stage filled with concert posters, artifacts, and photos from the venue's history.

JOIN THE CROWD
AT BEALE STREET MUSIC FESTIVAL

Kicking off the annual Memphis in May International Festival, Beale Street Music Festival is three days of live music on multiple stages during the first weekend in May. Held in Tom Lee Park along the riverfront of the Mississippi River, the event brings in thousands of people from around the region for music, food, and revelry each year.

The Beale Street Music Festival lineup has something for almost everyone, providing a mix of chart-topping artists and popular groups along with throwback bands, soul legends, and local artists of all genres. Gary Clark Jr., Cardi B, Smashing Pumpkins, and Weezer have all performed in recent years.

Also a part of the festivities, the Blues Stage on Beale features free blues concerts at Handy Park on Beale Street proper.

Tom Lee Park
Riverside Dr.
memphisinmay.org

33

BRING THE KIDS AND PETS
TO BARTOPIA AT RAILGARTEN

Parents know the struggle to find a spot that's both kid-friendly and grown-folks approved.That's why they invented Railgarten. The place is set up as an indoor-outdoor all ages hangout, with a full-fledged playground, a sand volleyball court, big screens, outside picnic-style seating and inside tables. You can even bring your dog, provided they're on a leash. The focal point of the yard is the stage, where local and visiting bands perform several times a week.

Order tropical-inspired cocktails and beer from the outdoor bars, where you can also order from the "garten menu" with burgers, sandwiches, and snacks that servers will bring over to your table. The attached restaurant, The Farmer, serves elevated Southern comfort food, wine, and cocktails.

2166 Central Ave.
901-504-4342
railgarten.com

TIP

Railgarten is family-friendly during the day and early evenings, but later evenings (or during ticketed concerts) the bar and yard have age restrictions, so check out the schedule before you go.

34

BEAT THE BLUES
AT THE INTERNATIONAL BLUES CHALLENGE

Witness the world's largest pilgrimage of blues music every year in Memphis at the annual International Blues Challenge (IBC). From every corner of the world come groups, duos, and solo blues artists, ready to croon for crowds and judges.

Usually held in January, the Blues Foundation hosts the IBC all week long in clubs concentrated on Beale Street, a series of qualifying performance competitions that lead up to the big event on Saturday at the Orpheum Theatre.

To enter, musicians must must have won their local Blues Foundation–affiliated competition in the previous year. There's also a youth artist showcase and an international showcase. Best of all, these competitions are open to the public—a wristband pass gets you in to every show, every night, or you can purchase a pass for just one evening.

blues.org

ROCK TO THE MUSIC
AT MEMPHO MUSIC FESTIVAL

Started in 2017, Mempho is a relatively newer three-day music festival that offers big-name acts in a chill, "good vibes only" festival environment. Unlike the sprawling festival grounds and high hype of other big-name fests, Mempho aims for an accessible, welcoming experience.

Usually held in September or early October at the Radians Amphitheater at the Memphis Botanic Garden, Mempho's past headliners have included Beck, Anderson .Paak, Cage the Elephant, Post Malone, The Raconteurs, Widespread Panic, and the Avett Brothers. Memphis bands have rounded out past years' lineups, from rapper Juicy J to rock favorites Lucero to legendary Stax group The Bar-Kays.

Up-and-coming artists grace the two stages as well, plus Mempho's Incendia experience caters to the dance music crowd. Memphis DJs turn it up under the flame-lit aura of the Incendia geodesic dome until late in the evening every night of the festival.

Radians Amphitheater
memphofest.com

36

WORSHIP SUNDAY MORNING WITH REVEREND AL GREEN

The "Let's Stay Together" and "Love and Happiness" Al Green of 1970s Royal Studios Memphis is alive and well in music compilations, albums, and recordings. Today's Al Green, however, is the Reverend Al Green, longtime pastor of the Full Gospel Tabernacle church. A Sunday morning service at the church is a popular activity for dedicated Memphis music pilgrims, but be prepared: it's an authentic worship session and sermon, not a concert.

Things get started at 11:30 a.m. sharp and the smooth-voiced former singer can preach into the late afternoon. A small but mighty gospel choir and seven-piece band start out the service before Reverend Green joins them in the pulpit. Silence your cell phone, drop a donation in the passed offering plate, and don't be afraid to clap and raise your own voice, if you're so moved.

787 Hale Rd.
901-345-8040

LISTEN LOCAL
AT MEMPHIS MUSIC VENUES

Where do the locals go for live music in Memphis? Tours come to FedExForum and the Orpheum, of course, but the city has a slew of beloved local venues that keep the music going every night of the week. The Hi-Tone Cafe has been a Memphis music experience in its various forms since 1998. Today's Hi-Tone, run by Brian "Skinny" McCabe, is the home for touring and local bands, art events, and comedy shows seven nights a week. Upstairs in the Big Room, catch all kinds of bands from metal to rap to punk; downstairs in the Small Room, hang out for intimate shows and mini-festivals.

Minglewood Hall in Midtown hosts 1,500-person concerts for touring bands and local artists. In the same complex, you'll find B-Side, a 100-person venue with a neighborhood bar feel—catch Thursday night bluegrass with Devil Train, a comedy show, or the Smiths cover band, Louder than Bombs.

Minglewood Hall/B-Side
1555 Madison Ave.
901-729-6114
minglewoodhallmemphis.com

Hi-Tone Cafe
282–284 N Cleveland St.
901-490-0335
hitonecafe.com

GET SPIRITED
AT EARNESTINE & HAZEL'S

When the jukebox starts playing randomly or you feel a cool draft sitting in an upstairs nook while you're at Earnestine & Hazel's, no need to worry. It's probably just the spirits who reside in the former-pharmacy-turned-brothel-turned-nightclub, and it's part of the experience.

A place that manages to be a local dive and a tourist magnet, E&H has received plenty of national press from ghost-hunting TV shows to profiles in *Esquire* magazine to "most haunted" lists.

The first floor has a long bar serving beer and soul burgers only, the aforementioned jukebox, a few booths, and pool tables up by the dusty front windows. Bands set up for live shows in the back by the narrow, creaky staircase.

Upstairs, things get spookier down a dimly lit hall with peeling paint (with side rooms full of random furniture and broken electronics) to the corner bar where you can order "the hard stuff" from longtime bartender Mr. Nate Barnes.

531 S Main St.
901-523-9754
earnestineandhazels.com

HEAR THE BACKSTORY
AT B.B. KING'S BLUES CLUB

Memphis Jones knows so much about music, he had to change his name. The musician is a staple on Beale Street, with regular performances of his Memphis music review at B.B. King's Blues Club. He and his band share the city's music history through his expert storytelling woven through songs with ties to Memphis. The show's medleys range from the Box Tops' "The Letter" to Mahalia Jackson's "Move On Up a Little Higher" to Neil Diamond's "Sweet Caroline," which, yes, was recorded in Memphis at American Sound Studio in 1969.

B.B. King's on Beale hosts live music almost every night, featuring blues and rock groups and soulful singers. For a fine dining experience, go up the "secret" street entrance to Itta Bena, the restaurant above B.B. King's.

143 Beale St.
901-524-5464
bbkingclubs.com

BOOGIE DOWN
AT PAULA & RAIFORD'S DISCO

Paula & Raiford's Disco doesn't get going until at least 10 p.m. and is only open on Friday and Saturday nights. By midnight, there's a line of people waiting to get in, standing behind the velvet ropes on a sidewalk red carpet. That's because Raiford's is the Memphis after-party spot—or usually, the after-party to the after-party.

Founded in 1976 by the late Robert Raiford, the club has seen multiple iterations through the years. Robert's daughter Paula Raiford runs the club these days, keeping her father's commitment to a positive party atmosphere with a pop and R&B playlist.

First-time visitors will experience sensory overload: there's a rainbow of neon lights, pulsing music, painted handprints on the walls, and glittering disco balls, all in a haze due to the fog machines. The best advice is to hydrate, bring cash, and wear your "boogie shoes" because everyone at Raiford's ends up on the dance floor eventually.

14 S 2nd St.
901-521-2494
paularaiford.com/home.html

41

HAIL A ROCKIN' RIDE:
TAKE A BACKBEAT TOUR

A vintage two-tone bus with a "Love and Happiness" sign pulls up to Alfred's on Beale and a gal with a guitar steps out to greet you. It's time to take the Memphis Mojo Tour, run by Backbeat Tours in Memphis.

Local musicians serve as energetic, funny tour guides on the 90-minute ride around town, sharing stories and telling tales, with a few musical interludes along the way. You'll see about 10 different landmarks and get the skinny on places like the Lorraine Motel and Elvis's childhood home.

Backbeat Tours also offers guided walking tours around the city. There's a historical tour, a ghost tour featuring haunted places, and their three-hour "Discovery" tour which includes a barbecue tasting and admission to either the Edge Motor Museum or the Memphis Rock 'n' Soul Museum.

197 Beale St.
901-527-9415
backbeattours.com

FedExForum
Courtesy of Unsplash

SPORTS AND RECREATION

HANG OUT IN NATURE
AT SHELBY FOREST

A few minutes north of Memphis proper, transport yourself to a wilderness wonderland and feel a full escape from the hustle and bustle of your everyday life. Meeman-Shelby Forest State Park is a gem in the Mid-South, and allows visitors and residents to explore the forests, lakes, and streams on top of the Chickasaw Bluff along the Mississippi River. Do you want to camp? Fish? Hike? Go on a nature trail? Find wildlife? Go horseback riding? Canoe? Play disc golf? Bike? You can do it all and more at Shelby Forest. From a relaxing picnic-and-playground day with the family to three- and four-mile hikes on the Woodland or Chickasaw Bluff Trails, make sure this place is a part of your Memphis adventures.

910 Riddick Rd., Millington
901-876-5215
tnstateparks.com/parks/meeman-shelby

TIP

If you need to stock up on snacks or just enjoy some amazing burgers on the deck, you must stop at Shelby Forest General Store, a Memphis institution.

CAMP, HIKE, OR SWIM WITH A SIDE OF HISTORY
AT T.O. FULLER STATE PARK

There's enough history to fill a book at T.O. Fuller State Park. First, about the park—it was the first park open for African Americans east of the Mississippi during segregation and it was renamed after prominent African American educator and leader Dr. Thomas O. Fuller in 1942. Long before that, Native Americans lived in the area, leaving behind earthen mounds and other artifacts discovered in the 1930s when park builders were digging a space for a swimming pool. Today there is the C.H. Nash Museum on the site of Chucalissa where people can visit to learn about these Mississippian peoples and archaeologists-in-training can work. The park itself offers hiking, camping, and a swimming pool—built in a different location than the mounds, which are still intact!

1500 W Mitchell Rd.
901-543-7581
tnstateparks.com/parks/t-o-fuller

TRAVERSE THE MISSISSIPPI
ON THE BIG RIVER CROSSING

At one mile long, Big River Crossing on the Harahan Bridge is the longest pedestrian crossing of the Mississippi River. You can walk or bike across and take in the one-of-a-kind views of the Memphis city skyline, including the unmissable Bass Pro Pyramid, the wooded floodplain on the Arkansas side, and the roaring waters of the rivers below. At night, you can enjoy the views of the Mighty Lights show both from the Harahan Bridge and the Hernando de Soto Bridge (sometimes called the "M" bridge) north of Big River Crossing. Both bridges are lit up in colors and patterns to honor various holidays, events, and historical moments. You can find out what tonight's colors mean by checking out Mighty Lights on social media.

Memphis side: Channel 3 Dr. and Virginia Ave.
Arkansas side: Bridgeport and Dacus Lake Roads
bigrivercrossing.com

TIP

From the Memphis side of the bridge, park on the street along Channel 3 Drive or in the lot at Martyrs Park; from the Arkansas side, park at Dacus Lake Road, which is accessible via Exit 1 on I-55.

CHEER ON
THE MEMPHIS GRIZZLIES

If you want to understand the culture of Memphis and fully absorb the locals' love for the city, you have to attend a Memphis Grizzlies NBA game at FedExForum. Some of basketball's biggest stars have worn the Grizzlies uniform—Ja Morant, Ziare Williams, Marc Gasol, Pau Gasol, Vince Carter, and Mike Conley Jr., to name just a few. In the arena, the energy is electric, the in-game entertainment stands out with humor and creativity that's unique to Memphis, and the gameplay will keep you on the edge of your seat. The entire experience is fun for dedicated and casual basketball fans alike, from pregame Grizz drumline action on Beale Street to WWE-inspired halftime shows with Grizz the mascot, to the best official (and unofficial) merch in the league. With the Memphis Grizzlies, the roster may change, but the "grit and grind" Memphis-loving spirit stays the same.

FedExForum
191 Beale St.
grizzlies.com

TAKE YOURSELF OUT
TO A BALL GAME

AutoZone Park in Downtown Memphis is home to two of our beloved teams: the Memphis Redbirds and the Memphis 901 FC soccer team. Since 1998 the Redbirds, a Triple-A feeder for the St. Louis Cardinals Major League Baseball team, have hit homers and caught fly balls to the delight of local fans. They even won the Triple-A National Championship in 2018. It's an amazing way to see future major leaguers learn the ropes. In 2019 the Memphis 901 FC soccer team (part of the USL Championship league) came to town, dazzling locals with team enthusiasm and the ballpark's ingenious switch from baseball to soccer pitch overnight. Both teams offer affordable tickets and up-close accessibility to professional athletes—and we can't forget the great ballpark food including the world-famous barbecue nachos.

AutoZone Park
200 Union Ave.
901-721-6000
memphis901fc.com
memphisredbirds.com

47

LOG 26.2 (OR CHEER)
AT THE ST. JUDE MEMPHIS MARATHON

It's arguably the biggest sporting event of the year in Memphis, when 25,000 people come from across the country to race for an amazing cause: the fight to cure childhood cancer. Every December, Memphis hosts the St. Jude Memphis Marathon that shuts down part of the city's streets and brings everyone outdoors to bundle up and cheer on these brave, hardworking runners. If you're not up for a full marathon, there's also a half-marathon, a 10K and a 5K; if you're not up for running at all, just join one of the lively cheering sections posted up between mile markers. The race travels through parts of Midtown and Downtown, including the St. Jude Children's Research Hospital campus, an undeniably special moment for runners and spectators alike.

stjudemarathon.org

CLIMB MEMPHIS ROX

When you think Memphis, you probably don't think "rock climbing" but at Memphis Rox in the Soulsville neighborhood, you'll find a community of climbers who understand the importance of accessibility in the sport. No matter your age, experience level, or ability to pay, Memphis Rox is here to teach climbing and bouldering, and to cheer you on your way up (and back down!). The gym is a pay-what-you-can situation with some suggested fees if you need an idea, but you will need to ask for help from a staffer if you want to climb the 45-foot top-rope climbing walls. Maybe start out with a bouldering wall that lets you try it out on your own with a soft mat for protection below you. Memphis Rox is just another unexpected and special reason to visit the Soulsville neighborhood in South Memphis.

879 E McLemore Ave.
901-401-6104
memphisrox.org

WANDER THROUGH THE OLD FOREST
AT OVERTON PARK

It's unusual for a forest to exist because of the Supreme Court, but in the Old Forest at Overton Park in Midtown, that's exactly the case. In the 1960s, plans were made to extend Interstate 40 through the middle of the city, straight through the 10,000-year-old ecosystem. Thankfully, the Citizens to Preserve Overton Park fought to protect the area in a case that went all the way to the Supreme Court and won. Today you can walk or bike on paved hard trails, soft trails, and dirt trails through the old forest growth; enjoy a stroll around Rainbow Lake; have a picnic; or pickup a game of wiffle ball on the Greensward.

1930 Poplar Ave.
901-214-5450
overtonpark.org

TIP

Play nine holes at the Overton Park 9 (formerly the Links at Overton), which reopened after a total renovation in summer 2022. Book your $10 tee time at overtonpark9.org.

BRING YOUR BOARD
TO THE SKATE PARK

If you're a skater looking for half-pipes, ledges, rails, banks, and bowls, Memphis has several skate parks that will be right up your alley. Tobey Park is the most established skate park in Memphis, an outdoor park that opened in 2011 in the Midtown area. Skaters of all levels are welcome, but the best time for kids who are just starting out is earlier in the morning, when they'll likely have the park to themselves.

Raleigh Springs skate park is a larger outdoor facility with a large bowl, banked wall, ledges, handrails, ramps, and more adjacent to a pond, a walking path, and the Raleigh Library.

Tobey Park
2599 Avery Ave.
memphisparks.com/park/tobey-park

Raleigh Springs Civic Center Skate Park
3384 Austin Peay Hwy.
memphisparks.com/park/raleigh-springs-civic-center

BE A KID AGAIN
AT THE CHILDREN'S MUSEUM

The Children's Museum of Memphis is a kids' dream come true. From hands-on science activities and indoor rock climbing to a vintage carousel and outdoor playground and splash park, it's the perfect place to bring the whole family. The little ones can run and play to their hearts' content in the unique candy-colored playground with a kid-sized zip line, merry-go-round, and more. The museum's exhibits and play areas include a dino dig, fire station, FedEx plane cockpit, kid-sized bank and grocery store, and a 50-foot Mississippi River model. There are special areas for kids ages 4 and under so they can get in on the fun, too. The Children's Museum is open Tuesday through Sunday except major holidays, and admission is a flat rate of $15 for kids ages 1 to 100.

2525 Central Ave.
901-458-2678
cmom.com

TIP

From Memorial Day to Labor Day, everyone can cool off at CMOM's outdoor H2Oh! Splash Park full of fountains, sprayers, misters, tunnels, and bubble makers.

EXPERIENCE NATURE
AT THE MEMPHIS BOTANIC GARDEN

With 96 acres of plants, trees, and pathways and 30 different specialty gardens, the Memphis Botanic Garden has plenty to occupy a leisurely afternoon of herbaceous exploration. Grown-ups will enjoy the finer points of the Japanese garden and many tree varieties, along with wine tastings, cultural programs, and concerts. The Herb Garden features more than 500 species of herbs and is one of the largest such collections in the country.

The kids will love the 2.6 acre progressive playground, My Big Backyard, with multicolored playhouses, a people-sized birdhouse, a mud-pie-making station, and "wormhole" tunnels. My Big Backyard has plenty of room for kids to run around on a grassy lawn—it's all about letting the little ones get their hands dirty. They'll also love feeding the fish at the koi pond and digging up "fossils" in the prehistoric plant area.

750 Cherry Rd.
901-636-4100
membg.org

TIP

The Memphis Botanic Garden hosts a Live at the Garden concert series with a show every month in summer and fall. You can bring your own picnic and enjoy big-name bands on tour.

DECIDE YOUR OWN ADVENTURE AT SHELBY FARMS PARK

Five times larger than New York City's Central Park, Shelby Farms Park is a 4,500-acre adventure brimming with outdoor activities. Canoe, kayak, paddleboard, or fish at Hyde Lake (one of the park's 20 lakes and ponds) or explore 40 miles of paved and unpaved trails through forests and fields—on foot or by bike. Go horseback riding, zip-line across Pine Lake at Go Ape Treetop Adventure course, or check out the resident buffalo herd. The Woodland Discovery Playground is the park's destination play area, where kids can crawl across a rope web, shoot down a 26-foot slide, and climb just about everything. Reserve a patio table for dinner at Coastal Fish Company in the park for an unforgettable sunset view over Hyde Lake.

6903 Great View Dr. N
901-222-7275
shelbyfarmspark.org

CYCLE THE CITY

If you want to ride your bike in Memphis, things are looking up! In the last decade, Memphis has added more than 270 miles of bike lanes and protected pathways throughout the city. Beginners will appreciate the paved Shelby Farms Greenline, a mostly straight shot 10 miles long through the middle of the city. It connects Overton Park in Midtown to Shelby Farms Park, which has its own trails as well. The Wolf River Greenway will be a 26-mile paved walk/bike path meandering along the Wolf River through the city; many portions of this greenway are complete, providing bikers with plenty of scenic byways to peddle.

For bikers of the mountain variety, check out the Stanky Creek Trails at Nesbit Park, the Tour de Wolf at Shelby Farms Park, or the Wolf River Trails in Germantown. Big River Trail offers 70 miles of riverside trails on the levee system, connecting the Big River Crossing in Downtown Memphis with Marianna, Arkansas, along the Mississippi River.

shelbyfarmspark.org/shelby-farms-greenline
wolfriver.org
bigrivertrail.com
stankycreek.com

TIP

If you need a little extra juice, Explore Bike Share offers electric bike rentals from docking stations around town.
explorebikeshare.bcycle.com

55

HORSE AROUND
AT THE GERMANTOWN CHARITY HORSE SHOW

You won't need a fancy hat or a special invitation to attend this annual equestrian event in Germantown, a suburb just outside of Memphis. You will need an appreciation for sportsmanship, horses, and a friendly disposition—this is the Germantown Charity Horse Show, a staple of the community for more than 75 years.

For five days in early June, equestrian professionals from near and far gather at the grounds for one of the oldest all-breed horse shows in the country. Strike up a conversation with fellow showgoers on the open bleachers on a summer night; if you're not a horse expert, one of them may be. They can likely tell you all about the hunter jumpers, carriage-driving competitions, and the mesmerizingly fast-footed Paso Fino horses. Leave the fancy outfits at home; standard attire is casual and heat-friendly like sundresses, hats, and shorts.

7745 Poplar Pike, Germantown
901-754-0009
gchs.org

56

PADDLE
THE WOLF RIVER

The Wolf River is Memphis's *other* major river, and paddling its waters through multiple ecosystems and sections needs to be on your bucket list. Find a local outfitter to rent you a canoe or kayak and gear, and to guide you through paddling this fascinating feat of conservation. The Ghost River section will take you through towering cypress-tupelo swamps, wetlands, forests, and the eerily placid Spirit Lake of the Upper Wolf. It's easy to get lost in the prehistoric-feeling swampland, so that guide or outfitter service (which can include shuttle service) is highly recommended. The Wolf River Conservancy's hard work has preserved the river and its watershed for generations of Memphians and visiting adventurers to enjoy.

Visit wolfriver.org/paddling for a list of local outfitters

Blues City Kayaks
901-762-1133
ande@bluescitykayaks.com

Kayak Memphis Tours
901-482-2942
kayakmemphis@outlook.com

Outdoors, Inc.
901-755-2271
customerservice@outdoorsinc.com

Wolf River Canoe Trips
901-877-3958

The Lorraine Motel and
National Civil Rights Museum
Photo courtesy of Flickr Commons

CULTURE AND HISTORY

SPEND THE DAY
ON BEALE STREET

Music and nightlife bring big energy to historic Beale Street every evening, but there's something to be said for exploring the city's most famous avenue during daylight hours. Start at the Beale Street blue neon arch for a photo opp, then walk over to the Elvis statue between Main and Second for more pictures. After that, stroll east (away from the river) to see the Brass Note Walk of Fame sidewalk that honors Memphis music legends. Stop into A.Schwab general store, which is only open during the day, or hang out in Handy Park in case there's a free daytime concert going.

Continue your walk to the Withers Collection, the bright blue W. C. Handy House where the "Father of the Blues" lived in the early 1900s, then on across Fourth Street to observe Robert Church Park, named for the South's first Black millionaire, and Ida B. Wells Plaza.

A.Schwab
163 Beale St.
901-523-9782
a-schwab.com

Beale Street Entertainment District
901-526-0115
bealestreet.com

TAKE A RIDE ON THE RIVER
WITH MEMPHIS RIVERBOATS

Take in panoramic Mississippi River views from the decks of a Memphis riverboat! You have a couple of options to experience the modern version of this 200-year-old tradition. Memphis Riverboats operates cruises that board from Beale Street Landing, where you can take a daytime sightseeing tour or an evening dinner cruise on the 100-foot-long, three-level *Island Queen* boat.

On the day tour, you'll take in great views and historical information from the friendly crew while cruising on a paddle wheel boat for about 90 minutes; the dinner cruise is two hours and includes a barbecue dinner and live music. The sightseeing excursion is offered daily from March through October, and on weekends in November, while the dinner cruise sails on weekends and special occasions. Advanced reservations are recommended.

If you want to make a further commitment to the riverboat experience, several companies offer overnight cruises that explore the Upper or Lower Mississippi River and stop in Memphis—look into American Cruise Lines or Viking Mississippi cruises.

45 S Riverside Dr.
901-527-2628
memphisriverboats.net

EXPLORE
THE MEMPHIS RIVERFRONT

The lovely views from the banks of the Mississippi River are only the beginning of what you can enjoy along the Memphis Riverfront. Start on the southern end at Martyrs Park. This picnic-perfect park is named "Martyrs Park" for the Memphians who stayed behind to help the sick during the 1878 yellow fever epidemic. There are views of the Harahan Bridge, parking, and plenty of trees. Continue on the Riverwalk, a marked, paved trail that meanders through the South Bluffs community. The Riverwalk connects all the parks along the riverfront, including Tom Lee Park and the River Garden at Mississippi River Park—a playground area filled with native plants. Between the two, you'll find the riverboat dock, Beale Street Landing, with its eye-catching grassy slope, colorful tower, and wind-powered 45-foot-tall sculptures.

Martyrs Park
Channel 3 Dr.
memphisparks.com/park/martyrs-park

Tom Lee Park
Riverside Dr.
memphisparks.com/park/tom-lee-park

Beale Street Landing
251 Riverside Dr.
memphisriverparks.org

River Garden at Mississippi River Park
51 Riverside Dr.
memphisparks.com/park/river-garden

CRUISE IN
TO THE EDGE MOTOR MUSEUM

Up the street from Sun Studio, the Edge Motor Museum stands as a testament to hot-rod culture in post–World War II Memphis. Built in the former St. Blues Guitar Factory in what's now called the Edge District, this strip was once known as "auto row" for its car dealerships and repair shops. Now, the museum showcases our love for the American sports car.

Inside you're guaranteed to see plenty of incredible classic cars in mint condition and to learn all about their history. It's not a personal car collection, but a carefully curated display of historic vehicles that's fun for everyone, even if you're not a motorhead yourself.

645 Marshall Ave.
901-441-2277
edgemotormuseum.com

TIP

While you're in the neighborhood, check out establishments like Inkwell cocktail bar and Flyway Brewing Memphis.

61

MEET THE DUCKS

BEFORE A PEABODY HISTORY TOUR

It's 11 a.m. at the historic Peabody Memphis hotel in Downtown Memphis, and a crowd gathers in the well-appointed lobby. Children line the red carpet that leads from the elevator to a marble fountain, and people watch from the mezzanine. What is all this pomp and circumstance for? The ducks, of course. Every day five North American mallards waddle into the elevator down from the roof—led by a highly qualified and well-dressed Duckmaster—then march straight across the lobby and flop into the fountain, where they happily splash around all day.

At 5 p.m. they march right back up to their Duck Palace for a cozy night's sleep.The Peabody Memphis hotel's feathered friends have delighted people from around the world for decades, but there's more to the story than meets the eye. You can take an hour-long history tour around the hotel by making advance reservations. The tour is $10 per person, but children 12 and under are free.

149 Union Ave.
901-529-4000
peabodymemphis.com

HONOR HISTORY
AT THE NATIONAL CIVIL RIGHTS MUSEUM

Built at the site of the assassination of Dr. Martin Luther King Jr. in 1968, the National Civil Rights Museum delves into civil rights struggles in Memphis and beyond. Immersive, life-size exhibits invite you to sit in at a lunch counter segregation protest or peer through the windows of a burned-out Freedom Ride bus replica.

The museum weaves together overarching stories of the civil rights movement and provides context for Dr. King's work in Memphis, culminating in visitor access to his hotel room, preserved as it was on the night before his death. The plaza is free to visit, which allows you to view the Lorraine Motel and the balcony, marked with a wreath, where Dr. King took his final steps. The museum also covers today's current civil rights struggles across the world, connecting past, present, and Memphis in one moving museum.

450 Mulberry St.
901-521-9699
civilrightsmuseum.org

TRACE MLK IN MEMPHIS
WITH A SELF-GUIDED TOUR

Trace Dr. King's experiences in Memphis before his death and you'll better understand the legacy of his work—and the labor and civil rights movements that continue today.

MLK Reflection Park: Dedicated during the 2018 MLK50 anniversary commemoration, the Reflection Park near Beale Street features sculptures, historical markers, and a reflection pool.

Echol Cole and Robert Walker Historical Marker: This somber location honors Echol Cole and Robert Walker, two Memphis sanitation workers whose deaths due to a garbage truck malfunction in 1968 sparked more than 1,000 of their coworkers and allies to go on strike for better working conditions. Dr. King visited Memphis shortly after to support this sanitation workers strike. The marker is in East Memphis at the corner of Sea Isle and Colonial Roads.

Clayborn Temple: This historic church in Downtown Memphis was a gathering place for the March 28, 1968, march to City Hall attended by Dr. King. Also see the adjacent I AM A MAN Plaza, honoring the members of the 1968 sanitation workers strike.

Mason Temple: This headquarters for the Church of God in Christ is where Dr. King gave his final "Mountaintop" speech the night before he was killed. You can drive by the site or contact the church directly at 901-947-9300 to see if tours are available.

ADD STOPS TO YOUR ITINERARY:

Memphis Heritage Trail
memphisheritagetrail.com/maps

United States Civil Rights Trail Memphis Sites
civilrightstrail.com/memphis

FOCUS ON BLACK HISTORY WITH A TOUR OF POSSIBILITIES

No self-guided tour or museum can substitute for the personal experience of a Tour of Possibilities. Founded by Carolyn Michael-Banks, this van tour gives small groups the chance to learn about African American history and culture from personal, knowledgeable, and entertaining guides as they're driven across the city or led via caravan.

A Tour of Possibilities (or "ATOP") focuses on Black history in Memphis and the accomplishments of Black Memphians. Carolyn or one of her trusted guides will point out landmarks such as the Slave Haven Underground Railroad Museum, the Mason Temple, or Royal Studios music recording studio that produced hits like Al Green's "Let's Stay Together" and Mark Ronson and Bruno Mars's "Uptown Funk." You may even be treated to a musical interlude (recorded or sung) by your guide.

901-326-3736
atopmemphis.com

GIVE BACK
AT ST. JUDE CHILDREN'S RESEARCH HOSPITAL

Memphis has plenty to be proud of, and being home to St. Jude Children's Research Hospital is at the top of that list. Founded in 1962 by entertainer Danny Thomas and named for the patron saint of hopeless causes, St. Jude's mission is to find cures for cancer and other childhood diseases.

Visitors can take a self-guided tour of the gold-domed Danny Thomas/ALSAC Pavilion on the hospital's campus to learn more about its founder and mission, open daily 8 a.m. to 4 p.m. with free admission. The Pavilion houses Thomas's memorabilia including his Emmy Awards and the Congressional Gold Medal. Its Mediterranean-inspired architecture, including the dome, geometric patterns, and Arabic inscriptions, are a nod to Thomas's Lebanese heritage.

In 2018, the hospital launched the St. Jude Global Alliance, providing training, resources, and education for institutions in nearly 60 countries to improve care and increase survival rates for children with childhood diseases worldwide.

262 Danny Thomas Pl.
901-595-4414
stjude.org

SEE THE HISTORIC HOMES
OF VICTORIAN VILLAGE

Adams Avenue in the 1800s was hopping! Then on the outskirts of town, wealthy Memphians filled the street with towering mansions in the hottest architectural styles of the day. Now that the city has grown up around and far beyond Victorian Village, visiting the area feels like time travel. Several of the homes were maintained, restored, or now function as museums or venues.

Mallory-Neely House: An 1852 Italianate villa, the Mallory-Neely house is one of the best-preserved Victorian-era homes in the country, with most of its original architectural features and decor still intact.

652 Adams Ave., moshmemphis.com

Woodruff-Fontaine House: The French Victorian mansion offers three floors of historic decor, architecture, and features like beautiful stained glass windows.

680 Adams Ave., woodruff-fontaine.org

James Lee House: Now operating as a luxurious bed-and-breakfast, the James Lee House underwent a miraculous nearly $2 million renovation in 2013–2014. While the James Lee House offers modern amenities, it still has its historic features and stunning architecture.

690 Adams Ave., jamesleehouse.com

WITNESS MEMPHIS HISTORY

AT THE SLAVE HAVEN UNDERGROUND RAILROAD MUSEUM

Located in a simple white house in Uptown, the museum is on property once owned by German immigrant Jacob Burkle. In 1855 he began offering shelter to people escaping slavery. At the museum, you'll see how these people may have hidden in a secret cellar and spent time at the house before continuing their journey north. Burkle operated this secret Memphis stop on the Underground Railroad until the abolition of slavery; in 1997, the home was restored and converted into a museum. For additional context on the cotton industry in Memphis, the Cotton Museum explores the role of enslaved people in harvesting cotton, sharecropping, the cotton industry's link to blues music, and the history of the building itself, once the home of the official Cotton Exchange—the stock market of cotton.

Slave Haven Underground Railroad Museum
826 N 2nd St.
901-527-7711
slavehavenmuseum.org

Cotton Museum
65 Union Ave.
901-531-7826
memphiscottonmuseum.org

GO WILD
AT THE MEMPHIS ZOO

Consistently named one of the top zoos in the United States, the Memphis Zoo's 70 acres of wildlife habitats and recreation areas bring in thousands of visitors every year. Located in Overton Park near the Overton Park Shell and the Old Forest, the zoo is home to more than 3,500 animals. See tigers, African lions, cheetahs, and jaguars in Cat Country; meet four hippos (Winnie, Binti, Splish, and Uzazi) at the Zambezi River exhibit. Grizzlies and black bears roam the Tetok Trek area, and black-footed penguins frolic and swim at Penguin Rock. Don't forget the elephants, giraffes, snakes, birds, Komodo dragons, primates, and many more.

When the weather's warm, take the family to the zoo's splash park, open May through September. In October, the zoo is open on select evenings for Zoo Boo's trick-or-treating and entertainment. During the holidays, celebrate with festive lights, a Ferris wheel, ice-skating rink, and more fun during Zoo Lights.

2000 Prentiss Pl.
901-333-6500
memphiszoo.org

TIP

To avoid crowds, skip the zoo in March when it's packed with kids on spring break. On Tuesdays from 2 p.m. until close, the zoo offers free admission to guests with a Tennessee ID. (There are no Free Tuesdays in March, though.)

WALK THROUGH HISTORY
AT ELMWOOD CEMETERY

If you see the word "cemetery" and think macabre or creepy, consider the fact that Elmwood Cemetery was established as a park in 1852 and is home to 1,500 majestic trees, colorful flowering plants, and shady spots for honoring Memphis history.

Hundreds of notable Memphians are buried here, including politicians, celebrities, soldiers, immigrants, and graves of the unknown. You can find the tomb of the South's first Black millionaire, Robert R. Church; you can find Union generals, brothel owner Emily Sutton, and monuments to the yellow fever victims of the 1870s. Elmwood offers a self-guided audio tour for $10 (CD or digital download) and maps for $5.

824 S Dudley St.
901-774-3212
elmwoodcemetery.org

TIP

For a schedule of docent-led seasonal tours, themed tours, and other events, visit the website.

70

PERUSE THE PINK PALACE

AT THE MUSEUM OF SCIENCE & HISTORY

There's plenty to do, see, and learn at the Museum of Science & History, including the Pink Palace Mansion built with pink marble by Piggly Wiggly magnate Clarence Saunders in the 1920s. Walk through permanent exhibits that explore natural history, Native American culture, and the Civil War through photos, fossils, and artifacts. See oddities like a miniature circus, a taxidermied polar bear, a shrunken head, and a life-size replica of the first Piggly Wiggly. There's also a planetarium and a giant screen theater, plus rotating exhibits on Memphis culture.

For years known as the Pink Palace Family of Museums, in 2021 the organization changed its name to the Museum of Science & History (or "MoSH") and continues to operate several attractions including the Central museum and Pink Palace Mansion, Lichterman Nature Center, and Mallory-Neely and Magevney Houses.

3050 Central Ave.
901-636-2362
moshmemphis.com

STEP BACK IN TIME
AT COLLIERVILLE'S DEPOT VISITOR CENTER

Step back in time at the picturesque Collierville Town Square, lined with unique shops, local restaurants, an historic train depot, a charming bandstand gazebo, and the Morton Museum of Collierville History. The museum explores 150 years of the town's history, including two 1863 Civil War battles, inside a restored Gothic Revival church.

Pop in to the Collierville Depot Visitors Center, an 1880s train depot that's home to the tourism office's headquarters and a gift shop. The whole family will appreciate the square's collection of historic trains that you can explore inside and out. This includes the iconic Frisco 1351 steam locomotive, a business train car, and a 1940s red caboose.

196 N Main St., Collierville
901-457-2650
colliervillemuseum.org
mainstreetcollierville.org

TIP

There are plenty of local restaurants, shops, and boutiques for dining and shopping nearby, plus seasonal events like a summer concert series and Christmas in Collierville.

UNCOVER THE SECRETS
OF THE CRYSTAL SHRINE GROTTO

You'd never expect to find a place like the Crystal Shrine Grotto in the middle of Memphis, and certainly not in the middle of a cemetery—but its unexpected beauty and strangeness is why this place is so memorable. Mexican artist Dionicio Rodriguez built the above-ground cave and other structures at Memorial Park Cemetery in the 1930s and 1940s.

The grotto is made from finished concrete made to look like rocks, boulders, or wood features. Walk inside and you'll find yourself in a cave lined with glittering crystals, shiny quartz, stalactite sculptures, and biblical folk art. Colorful lighting adds to the effect of an otherworldly experience. Nearby is the artist's *Abraham's Oak*, a towering tree sculpted from faux-finished cement. Walk through Memorial Park's gardens, footpaths, and bridges to see pools and water features including Rodriguez's *Fountain of Youth* among the peaceful memorials and graves.

5668 Poplar Ave.
901-302-9980
memorialparkfuneralandcemetery.com

VISIT
THE IDA B. WELLS STATUE

Head east past the bright lights of Beale Street, and you'll find a piece of history at the Ida B. Wells Plaza. Installed in 2021, the plaza honors the work of Ida B. Wells, an anti-lyching activist, journalist, and suffragette who fought for Black women's right to vote. She lived in Memphis for 16 years in the late 1800s, where she published the *Memphis Free Speech* newspaper. Still standing next to the plaza, the Beale Street Baptist Church provided offices for her paper, which was destroyed by an angry mob in 1892 in retaliation for publishing anti-lyching journalism.

At the plaza, you'll find several pavilions, a life-size statue of Wells created by local sculptors Andrea and Larry Lugar, and the *Tree of Strange Fruit* sculpture that memorializes lynching vicitims she honored in her work. Plans are in the works to enhance and expand the plaza in the coming years.

Beale and 4th Streets
idabwellsmemphis.org

LEARN ABOUT METALWORKING AT THE COUNTRY'S METAL MUSEUM

While you'll find plenty of amazing river views in Memphis, the Metal Museum offers some of the best glimpses of the Mississippi River in town. South of Downtown in the French Fort area—also the site of the Chickasaw mounds and Marine Hospital—this tucked-away campus is unique. Home to a museum, gallery space, an outdoor sculpture garden, and a blacksmith forge, the Metal Museum is the only institution in the country dedicated exclusively to fine metalworking.

In the coming years, the Metal Museum plans to expand their gallery and education spaces into the historic Rust Hall building in Overton Park, former home to the Memphis College of Art. Make a note to plan a future visit once the museum's expansion is open!

374 Metal Museum Dr.
901-774-6380
metalmuseum.org

TIP

The Metal Museum hosts regular public events like Whet Thursday, an after-hours open house with food, drinks, and metalsmithing demos, and the annual Repair Days, when people bring metal items to be fixed up by the pros at the museum.

EXPERIENCE BROADWAY
AT THE ORPHEUM

Where Broadway meets Beale Street! The historic Orpheum Theatre hosts traveling Broadway shows, world-class concerts, dance companies, and other performances throughout the year. In any given season, expect a mix of classic musicals, award-winning productions, and the most popular shows on their first national tours. Experience the glamour of the gilded ceilings, lush scarlet carpet, and glittering Czechoslovakian crystal chandeliers when you attend a show at the Orpheum.

Occasional backstage tours are offered for $10 per person for guests 6 and up—contact the Orphuem for the latest schedule. On the tour, you'll learn about the history of the theater, see the colorful murals painted backstage by traveling Broadway casts, and hear about the spectral residents of the theater, including a friendly ghost named Mary. Next door, the Halloran Centre hosts even more live music, entertainment, and theater.

203 S Main St.
901-525-3000
orpheum-memphis.com

GALLERY HOP
TO TONE MEMPHIS

Headquartered in the historic African American neighborhood of Orange Mound, TONE Memphis aims to elevate the art and experience of Black artists through exhibition of photography, paintings, sculpture, film, music, and more. TONE also hosts annual Juneteenth celebration events, including a fashion-focused dinner and gala and a community festival in the Orange Mound community. Like TONE, other independent art galleries thrive in diverse Memphis neighborhoods.

The Urevbu Contemporary gallery displays work from artists of the African diaspora and has been a long-standing part of the South Main Arts District. Also in South Main, the Jack Robinson Gallery showcases vintage photography from the eponymous artist who captured 1960s pop culture icons. In Cooper-Young, longtime Memphis art advocate Jay Etkin operates a gallery focused on contemporary artists, in addition to a vintage African art collection.

TONE Memphis
2234 Lamar Ave.

Urevbu Contemporary
410 S Main St.

Jack Robinson Gallery
44 S Huling
robinsongallery.com

Jay Etkin Gallery
942 S Cooper St.

77

GO BEHIND A LEGENDARY LENS
AT THE WITHERS COLLECTION

The most prolific photographer of the Civil Rights Movement, Memphian Dr. Ernest C. Withers captured millions of images during his 60-year career. His family, including his daughter Rosalind Withers, now manage the Withers Collection Museum & Gallery on Beale Street. The collection is open Tuesday through Sunday afternoons starting at noon, and you can reserve a docent-led tour by contacting the museum ahead of time.

During your visit, take in photography covering Negro League baseball; portraits of music legends like B.B. King, Isaac Hayes, and Ray Charles; and daily life for African Americans in Memphis, as well as photos from difficult moments in history—segregation, civil rights protests, many images of Dr. Martin Luther King Jr., and the 1955 trial of 14-year-old lynching victim Emmett Till.

333 Beale St.
901-523-2344
thewitherscollection.com

TIP

"You may need an hour to see the collection and many more to process what you've seen."—Samantha Crespo, author of *100 Things to Do in Memphis Before You Die, 1st–3rd Editions*

EXPERIENCE WHERE ART LIVES AT CROSSTOWN CONCOURSE

Once a Sears distribution center, as of 2017 this completely renovated "vertical urban village" Crosstown Concourse is a must-visit for Memphians and tourists. Start with the architecture. There's a million square feet of towering atriums filled with natural light, original columns, and an art deco tower; then move on to the art and attractions. Spend a few hours exploring the shops, art galleries, and the Listening Lab's thousands of albums. Catch a concert at the Crosstown Theater or the Green Room at Crosstown Arts, then grab a drink at the speakeasy-style Art Bar at Crosstown or one of the half-dozen restaurants in the building.

The neighborhood offers plenty to do as well; nearby you'll find Crosstown Brewing's taproom, Flip Side pinball bar, Black Lodge Video, and the Hi Tone Cafe music venue.

1350 Concourse Ave.
901-203-8300
crosstownconcourse.com

SMILE
FOR AMURICA!

Memphis photographer Jamie Harmon's Amurica Photobooth (and the photos taken within) are iconic. There's the signature interior of the silver teardrop trailer, wallpapered with colorful postcards, every inch covered with twinkling lights. Then there's the collection of quirky props, including hats of every style, muppets, mannequins, wigs, baby dolls, plastic animals, and a big American flag. Taking an Amurica photo, whether silly or faux-serious, inside one of Harmon's trailers is a Memphis rite of passage. Find the stationary setup inside Crosstown Concourse or rent one out for an event. If you can't get a photo for yourself, check out Jamie's incredible photo book, *Memphis Quarantine*, a collection of images captured during the early months of the 2020 coronavirus pandemic featuring hundreds of families and households in Memphis, available at memphisquarantine.com.

1350 Concourse Ave.
amurica.com

TELL YOUR TALE
AT SPILLIT MEMPHIS

Started in 2012 by Memphian Leah Keys, Spillit Memphis is a unique storytelling event where speakers and listeners connect while sharing true tales from their lives. Under the leadership of Creative Director Josh Campbell, these events are held throughout the year and are open to the public at different venues around Memphis. Many Spillit events are at Black Lodge Video in the Crosstown neighborhood.

At Center Stage events, storytellers submit their themed stories ahead of time and present the workshopped anecdotes at the event. For Spillit Slams, anyone in the audience can stand up on a whim and tell a five-minute tale—silly, sad, or strange—and the listeners vote on the best story. Whether you just wish to listen or are inspired to share your own, Spillit storytelling events are full of surprising moments and are a Memphis must-do.

spillitmemphis.org

BEHOLD A MEMPHIS MASTER AT THE BROOKS MUSEUM

For more than 105 years, the Memphis Brooks Museum of Art has hosted fine arts exhibits, events, and permanent installations at their home in Overton Park. The oldest and largest art museum in Tennessee, the Brooks has plans to move to a new, state-of-the-art building on the riverfront in Downtown Memphis in the mid-to-late 2020s.

In the meantime, visitors and art lovers can still explore the current location's permanent collections of art—European, contemporary, African Diaspora, and the Carroll Cloar Gallery. The latter is dedicated to the eponymous Memphis-based Southern painter and boasts one of the largest and best collections of his paintings.

Local art exhibitions, traveling installations, and community events round out the programming at the Brooks Museum. The museum's cafe, Feast and Graze, serves gourmet sandwiches, salads and meat and cheese snack plates.

1934 Poplar Ave.
901-544-6200
brooksmuseum.org

82

LET THE MUSIC FLOW
AT OPERA MEMPHIS'S 30 DAYS OF OPERA

Does opera seem inaccessible, esoteric, or even stuffy? Not so in Memphis, where the talented singers and patrons of Opera Memphis explore myriad ways to connect this beautiful art form with locals and visitors. The height of this pursuit is 30 Days of Opera, a month of free pop-up performances from Opera Memphis company members and guest artists. Usually held in the spring, catch these short songs or mini-shows at playgrounds, farmers markets, malls, and dog parks.

Enjoy innovative takes on classic operas and community-driven opera experiences hosted by Opera Memphis throughout the rest of the year. A few examples—*The Mikado* reenvisioned to include appearances from Pikachu and Godzilla; a pairing of the classic Donizetti *Pygmalion* with *The Companion* as a modern exploration of love in the Tinder age, or *Craigslistlieder*, an opera with lyrics based on real Craigslist ads.

901-202-4533
operamemphis.org

83

STAND AND APPLAUD
IN OVERTON SQUARE'S THEATER DISTRICT

The creativity and talent of Memphis comes alive on stage at the city's many theaters, including those in the Overton Square Theater District. With the Memphian boutique hotel, more than a dozen restaurants, and several live-music venues, Overton Square is the perfect area for a romantic evening or group outing.

Hattiloo Theatre is the only Black repertory theater in the region, dedicated to original works, musicals, and iconic shows created by Black playwrights about the Black experience.

Playhouse on the Square is the city's professional resident theater company, with three stages at Playhouse, Circuit Playhouse, and TheatreWorks @ The Square, respectively. Talented performers bring to life your favorite musicals, dramatic performances, off-Broadway hits, and original works.

Ballet Memphis's headquarters in Overton Square offers the city's professional ballet company rehearsal, performance, and classroom spaces. Catch a ballet at their headquarters, the nearby Playhouse on the Square, or other local venues.

Hattiloo Theatre
37 S Cooper St.
901-525-0009
hattiloo.org

The Circuit Playhouse
51 S Cooper St.
901-726-4656
playhouseonthesquare.org

Playhouse on the Square
66 S Cooper St.
901-726-4656
playhouseonthesquare.org

TheatreWorks @ The Square
2085 Monroe Ave.
901-726-4656
playhouseonthesquare.org

MAKE MOVIE MAGIC
WITH INDIE MEMPHIS

Indie Memphis Film Festival is a chance to see award-winning movies, short films, documentaries, and art house masterpieces before they go big. In 2022, Indie Memphis celebrated the 25th anniversary of the festival, held annually in October. For a week, Memphis hosts more than 100 screenings, panels, and events at multiple theaters around town. There's also a Black Creators Forum, virtual screenings, and after-parties where you can mingle with filmmakers.

Jurors bestow awards for Best Narrative Feature, Best Documentary Feature, Hometowner Feature (a Memphis-made film), Emerging Filmmaker, Audience Favorite, and more. If you aren't in town for Indie Memphis's fall festival you can always catch other screenings and events throughout the year. Indie Memphis also focuses on artist development, offering education, film grants, and other support for our local and student film communities.

901-214-5171
indiememphis.org

MAKE A MASTERPIECE
OR A MESS AT THE ART PROJECT

At the Art Project studio in Overton Square, kids can register for classes to build a dollhouse from cardboard, mix up some "slime," or learn art basics. But they will really love the Art Free Play sessions where they can go nuts with glitter, paint, and all the messy things parents appreciate remaining in the studio. Simply reserve your space ahead of time (it's $18 for 90 minutes of nonstructured class time), and parents can hang out while the young artists create to their hearts' content.

There are always small tables with mini projects like thumbprint animal drawings or kinetic sand sculptures if the kid wants a little more direction. Adults can get in on the artistic action with grown-up paint 'n' sip classes.

2092 Trimble Pl.
901-425-3434
artprojectmemphis.com

86

MEET
AT THE RAINBOW STREET MURAL

The Cooper-Young neighborhood has been known as the artsy, funky, forward-thinking area of Memphis for decades. Staples of the area include Goner Records, First Congo Church, Burke's Book Store, House of Mews, Java Cabana, and the Beauty Shop, while newer spots bring a fun and fresh vibe to the area—Cooper-Young Gallery, Buff City Soap, Hammer & Ale (where you can try flights of local beers), Memphis Whistle, and Knifebird wine bar.

In 2020, a group of local activists painted the first rainbow crosswalk in the state of Tennessee at the intersection of Cooper and Young, and in 2022 added the colorful symbol of LGBTQIA acceptance on all additional crossings in the intersection. Explore Cooper-Young for shopping, eating, and spending time where the locals do.

Cooper St. and Young Ave.
cooperyoung.com

WITNESS

MEMPHIS DANCE ONSTAGE

Memphis is home to vibrant dance companies offering classical and contemporary works in performances throughout the year. Change up the routine with New Ballet Ensemble's original show, *NutRemix*, a creative interpretation of the *Nutcracker* story that incorporates hip-hop, African dance, flamenco, and Memphis jookin' dance styles alongside traditional ballet.

Collage Dance teaches the next generation of diverse dancers on Broad Avenue; conservatory students often perform alongside professional company members in original work and special performances. Though founded in New York City, today's collective focus is influenced by the culture and history of Memphis.

Since 1986, Ballet Memphis has provided world-class dancers a chance to delight Memphis audiences. Each season offers classic repertory ballets such as *Cinderella* and *The Nutcracker*, along with seasonal programs with guest choreographers and contemporary original works.

New Ballet Ensemble & School
newballet.org

Collage Dance
collagedance.org

Ballet Memphis
balletmemphis.org

VIEW THE BLOOMS
AT THE DIXON GALLERY & GARDENS

With 17 acres of gardens and indoor gallery spaces, the Dixon provides a tranquil and colorful respite from the city in East Memphis. Every spring, tens of thousands of tulips bloom in yellows, pinks, reds, and purples across the grounds, but the gardens are teeming with lush plants and contemporary sculptures year-round.

Inside, see works from French Impressionists and Postimpressionists in the permanent collection, plus a variety of different exhibitions in painting and photography, including works from local artists, on display. There's a wonderful café and gift shop inside for after you're done exploring. The Dixon hosts regular events and programming, from parties to food trucks to tastings, so there are plenty of ways to enjoy this essential Memphis attraction. The Dixon offers free admission.

4339 Park Ave.
901-761-5250
dixon.org

GO BACK IN TIME
AT THE TIME WARP DRIVE-IN

It's a blast from the past every week at the Malco Summer Drive-In theater—one of the few drive-in outdoor movie theaters still around in the US. But you can really go back in time during the monthly Time Warp Drive-In. Organized by Black Lodge Video, Malco Theatres, Guerrilla Monster Films, Piano Man Pictures, and Holtermonster, this event is all about the cult classics, favorite films from your childhood, and notorious horror flicks. Fill up your car or truck with as many people as you can fit (it's a flat $25 fee), bring your lawn chairs, and set up for two or three movies starting at sundown and sometimes going late into the evening. A few past Time Warps include an *Indiana Jones* night, a *Child's Play* night with two *Chucky* movies, and an *Evil Dead* marathon.

Time Warp Drive-In
facebook.com/timewarpdrivein

Malco Summer Drive-In
5310 Summer Ave.
901-767-4320
malco.com/cinemas/summer-drive-in

The Bass Pro Shops Pyramid
Courtesy of Unsplash

SHOPPING AND FASHION

90

SPEND A DAY
ON BROAD AVENUE

You can spend a fun and funky day on Broad Avenue in the Binghampton neighborhood, near Overton Park. A perfect place to find a very Memphis souvenir, Broad Avenue is home to local gift and art shops like Falling Into Place, City & State, Mbabazi House of Style, and T Clifton Art Gallery. After shopping, choose from a unique variety of local restaurants including the modern diner The Liquor Store, farm-to-table Bounty on Broad, Memphis classic Broadway Pizza, or a romantic tapas and wine night at Maximo's on Broad. Treat yourself to boba or ice cream at Sugar Ghost, cupcakes at Muddy's Bake Shop, coffee at City & State, or local beers at Wiseacre Brewing's original location. Finish the night with a craft cocktail at pirate-themed pub The Cove—they often host live music or karaoke.

broadavearts.com

MIX IT UP
AT MBABAZI HOUSE OF STYLE

Started in 2005 by Grace Byeitima in Uganda, Mbabazi House of Style creates modern clothing made with traditional African textiles. The line is named after Byeitima's mother, Mbabazi Loy Rujumba. In 2014, Grace moved to Memphis and opened a shop on Broad Avenue. You can find vibrant, colorful clothing and accessories for women and children in the store, from dresses to jewelry to bags to scarves.

Mbabazi showcases items designed and created by Ugandan women at the production facility that Grace's mother still operates. The shop offers a range of sizes and even creates custom garments by commission. In addition to being a fair-trade business, Mbabazi offers fair living employment and apprenticeships to their employees.

2553 Broad Ave.
901-303-9347
mbabazistyles.com

ACE FIVE IN ONE SOCIAL CLUB'S
KINDERGARTEN FOR GROWN FOLKS

For unique and creative souvenirs, Five in One Social Club is one of the best places to shop around town. After many years on Broad Avenue, the artist-run shop moved around the corner to a bigger, brighter space for retail and classes.

That's because in addition to a ton of Memphis-made merch, the "kindergarten for grown folks" studio also offers fun workshops where adults can craft while sipping craft beer and meet other artsy grown-ups. For example, attendees can make stained glass suncatchers, create glasses from recycled wine bottles, weave a rope basket, or dye something with indigo.

On the retail side, shop screen-printed T-shirts, funky jewelry, original art prints, candles, and more, created mostly by local artists. Not everything is Memphis-themed, but if you're seeking a keepsake from the 901, Five in One is where it's at.

2575 Summer Ave.
901-308-2104
fiveinone.org

TAKE IT TO THE TOP
AT THE BASS PRO PYRAMID

It's true, Memphis is home to the world's sixth-largest pyramid! Built in the '90s as an event venue for concerts and sporting events, the steel-and-glass structure reopened in 2015 as a Bass Pro Shops megastore and Big Cypress Lodge luxury hotel. Throw out your notions of a bait shop or outdoor supply store; this place offers everything from camping gear to clothing to cooking supplies to toys.

The main floor features aquariums, an alligator tank, a bowling alley and restaurant, a fudge shop, and a display of boats and ATVs for sale. Spend some time exploring all the goods and gear, then ride the country's tallest freestanding elevator to the top for incomparable views on the glass-floored observation deck. The 28-story ride is $8 for adults, $5 for kids.

1 Bass Pro Dr.
901-291-8200
basspro.com/pyramid

TIP

Visit the Ducks Unlimited Waterfowling Heritage Center museum on the pyramid's second floor to see an extraordinary collection of antique duck decoys, calls, and taxidermy.

SOUP UP YOUR STYLE
AT STOCK & BELLE IN SOUTH MAIN

Stock & Belle is a stylish boutique in the South Main Arts District in Downtown Memphis that offers plenty of clothing, jewelry, gifts, art, and home goods, including modern furniture and unique decor. You can find women's and men's apparel, including Memphis-themed shirts along with a curated collection of locally made goods from local artisans, including souvenirs and gifts.

Continue on your shopping journey in the neighborhood at other nearby stores like Feelin' Memphis, with its local art and Memphis-themed gifts. There's plenty of public art to peruse and a plethora of food and drink options, from Elvis-era diner vibes at The Arcade Restaurant to upscale French dining at Bishop.

Stock & Belle
387 S Main St.
901-734-2911
stockandbelle.myshopify.com

Feelin' Memphis
509 S Main St.
901-800-1488
feelin-memphis.com

South Main Book Juggler
548 S Main St.
901-249-5370
southmainbookjuggler.com

Bishop
545 S Main St., Ste. 111 (inside Central Station)
901-896-0228
bishopmemphis.com

Arcade Restaurant
540 S Main St.
901-526-5757
arcaderestaurant.com

BROWSE THROUGH HISTORY AT A.SCHWAB

Step into living history on Beale Street at A.Schwab general store, where the motto is, "If we don't have it, you don't need it!" Established in 1876—making it the oldest store in the city—the current iteration of A.Schwab is part souvenir shop, part old-fashioned soda fountain, and part museum.

Only open during the day, A.Schwab general store sells vintage items, funky gifts, souvenirs, and Memphis music on vinyl. Whether you're seeking a sequined Elvis-themed mug, a cool T-shirt to commemorate your visit, or just a jar of pickles, the general store has you covered.

Be sure to peruse the "Beale Street Museum" section of A.Schwab with photos and artifacts from the store's history, then head over to the counter for a milkshake, an ice cream sundae, or even a boozy milkshake.

163 Beale St.
901-523-9782
a-schwab.com

DRESS LIKE A KING (OR QUEEN) AT LANSKY BROS.

When Bernard Lansky switched his Beale Street army surplus clothing store into a high-fashion men's boutique in the late 1940s, it was the first step to becoming an iconic Memphis store that dressed the new rock 'n' rollers of the '50s and '60s, including a young Elvis Presley, Johnny Cash, and Carl Perkins, among others.

The brand is still owned by the family and operated by Bernard's son Hal and his granddaughter Julie. Lansky's is located in the lobby of the Peabody Memphis, where they offer several fashion lines, including "Lansky Bros. Clothier to the King," with its signature 1950s-inspired clothing and reproductions from Elvis's wardrobe. The shop also has a modern women's line of luxury clothing as well as souvenirs and gifts themed for Memphis and the Peabody Memphis. There's also an online store.

149 Union Ave. (in the Peabody Memphis lobby)
901-529-9070
lanskybros.com

ROCK OUT
WITH GONER RECORDS

Blues, rock, and soul might have put Memphis music on the map, but Goner Records has held down an alternative rock presence in the city for 20 years. Goner, founded and run by Eric Friedl and Zac Ives, is a label, a store, and an annual festival. At the physical shop, you can find classic, current, old, new, and used LPs, 45s, CDs, books, magazines, and merch from all kinds of bands. The Goner label releases albums from local and international groups.

Every fall, Goner hosts the annual Gonerfest, which is like a Midtown Memphis Christmas for all manner of rock bands. Punk, garage, indie, ska, grunge, metal, and more—it's all a part of the four-day marathon music event, held since 2021 at Railgarten's indoor-outdoor music venue.

2152 Young Ave.
901-722-0095
goner-records.com

98

UNCOVER VINYL AT
SHANGRI LA RECORDS

Vinyl is back in a big way, and Memphis has multiple record stores to keep your albums spinning and music, new and old, in your ears. Shangri-La Records is one such place that has served music lovers since the late '80s.

In a cozy 120-year-old renovated house in Midtown, you'll find the shop completely packed with new and used vinyl, CDs, and merch from thousands of artists. Shangri-La buys used records, too. Pick up the latest popular releases or discover your new favorite Memphis band in the overflowing "local artists" section. The best part is the staff, most of whom are musicians themselves who are more than happy to talk tunes with you and help you find whatever you need.

1916 Madison Ave.
901-274-1916
shangri.com

SWAGGER INTO
HEWLETT & DUNN BOOT & CLOTHING CO.

The creak of worn wooden floors and the earthy smell of leather invite you into a store that has a nostalgic feel but offers the latest styles in leather goods and more. Since 1961, Hewlett & Dunn's family-owned store has been a mainstay of the historic Collierville town square shopping district.

While cowboy boots for men and women are the staple item, they also carry other leather items like bags, hats, and belts, as well as denim and other apparel. Shop for gifts and other locally made goods, or talk to the knowledgeable staff. There's a collection of antique radios, old-fashioned signage, and other items from the store's 60-year history to check out. If you're in the market for a pair of custom-designed and custom-fitted cowboy boots, Hewlett & Dunn offers this as well.

111 N Center St., Collierville
901-853-2636
hewlettdunn.com

TIP

Caffeinate before boot shopping at Square Beans coffeehouse next door to Hewlett & Dunn.

READ LOCAL
AT MEMPHIS'S INDIE BOOKSTORES

Shop local for books, from national bestsellers to local guidebooks, at Burke's Book Store, nestled on the strip in Cooper-Young. Burke's opened Downtown in 1875 (meaning it's one of the oldest independent bookstores in the South) and moved around town before landing in its current cozy location in 2007. Owners Cheryl and Corey Mesler and their team keep the shop stocked with new and used books specializing in Southern literature and even some hard-to-find volumes. You'll feel like you're stepping back in time as you peruse the shelves and check in each season to see the latest creative front-window display.

In East Memphis, Novel bookstore's current iteration provides shelves upon shelves of new books across genres—children's, young adult, novels, nonfiction, Memphis interest, and self-help—plus plenty of magazines, gifts, and locally made items.

Burke's Book Store
936 S Cooper St.
901-278-7484
burkesbooks.com

Novel
387 Perkins Extd.
901-922-5526
novelmemphis.com

The Memphis Zoo
Courtesy of Unsplash

SUGGESTED ITINERARIES

HISTORY BUFFS

FAMILY FRIENDLY

DATE NIGHT

TAKE IN A SHOW

TIME TO GET ARTSY

The Orpheum Theatre
Courtesy of Unsplash

Memphis Bridge
Courtesy of Unsplash

ACTIVITIES
BY SEASON

SPRING

SUMMER

FALL

WINTER

INDEX

Beale Street
Courtesy of Pixabay